Leadership

A Leadership And Motivational Book Focusing On
Primal Leadership And Self-deception

(Learn Communication Skills)

Reginald Brousseau

TABLE OF CONTENT

Chapter 1: How To Enhance Emotional Intelligence 1

Chapter 2: How To Complete Employment Application... 9

Chapter 3: Why Is Leadership So Indispensable? ..14

Chapter 4: Leadership Qualities To Adopt 26

Chapter 6: Types Of Leadership................................... 44

Chapter 7: Leadership Variations Administrative Authority 50

Chapter 8: Communication.. 54

Chapter 9: Balance And The Importance Of Self-Care 62

Chapter 10: Qualities Of Leadership 65

Chapter 11: Some Qualities Of A Genuine Leader .72

Chapter 12: Adapting To Change: The Importance Of Assessing And Modifying Your Objectives........... 81

Chapter 13: Mission Of A Leader 97

Chapter 14: Advantages And Disadvantages.......... 102

Chapter 15: Is Leadership An Easy Task? 106

Chapter 16: Fundamentals For Creating A Healthy Corporate Culture 118

Chapter 17: The New Assessment Tool 121

Chapter 1: How To Enhance Emotional Intelligence

Similar to self-assurance, emotional intelligence can be developed and enhanced over time. So let's commence with a few EQ-boosting tips and tricks!

Look Inward

Monitoring your own emotions and responses (as well as how they influence your decisions and behavior) can help you develop emotional intelligence and self-control. For instance, if you are feeling anxious or agitated, you may find yourself being abrupt with others or tensing your shoulders. Identifying these emotions and resulting behaviors enables you to find more effective alternatives or solutions for relieving your tension.

Practice Consciousness

Observing the emotions, behaviors, and interactions of those around you is equally essential for enhancing your emotional intelligence and ability to empathize with others as developing self-awareness. Additionally, your observations of others can help you communicate with and respond appropriately to them.

Accept Accountability for Your Emotions

Your emotions and actions originate from you, so it is essential to accept responsibility for how you conduct yourself and others. For instance, if you end up taking out your stress and frustrations on a coworker or employee, you may need to take a break to collect yourself, assess your emotions and behavior, and then respond appropriately (by apologizing to the employee or coworker and finding more effective stress management techniques).

Discover from Your Errors

Mistakes are inevitable, so the best we can do is to attempt to learn from them, prevent them from occurring again, and resolve any resulting conflicts.

Challenge Your Opinions and Ideas

It is simple to find yourself in a "echo chamber" where your thoughts, opinions, ideas, and beliefs are not challenged but instead reinforced by others. As a result, taking the time to comprehend diverse viewpoints and perspectives can help you better comprehend others, be receptive to new ideas, and possibly alter your own opinions or mindset. Keep in mind that learning is a process!

Recognize the Positive

Reflecting on and appreciating victories, successes, and positive moments in your personal and professional lives can also help you increase your emotional intelligence. You can also surmount your insecurities, strengthen your relationships with others, and become more resilient by doing so.

Determine Your Motivations

Take the time to identify and comprehend all of the factors that motivate you to conclude the race. This also serves as a reminder to persevere when you lose motivation while working on a project or pursuing a professional objective.

Know When to Simplify

It is admirable to constantly work on bettering yourself and pursuing your objectives, but you must also recognize when you (and your body) need a break.

Whether you practice yoga or read a book, escapism can (in moderation) do marvels for your overall health.

Recognize Your Emotional Triggers.

Recognizing your emotions as they occur can assist you in identifying the situations that elicit both positive and negative emotions. In addition, being aware of these stressors enables you to anticipate situations that may or do cause you stress, as well as foresee how you may react to future (negative or positive) situations. This can also help you feel more emotionally in control.

Focus on Your Physical Gestures

Nonverbal communication not only conveys your thoughts and feelings, but it can also affect how others perceive you. For instance, you may not be verbalizing your emotions, but your body language (such as a deeper, harsher tone of voice and a lack of eye contact) conveys that you are stressed or furious.

Engage in Active Listening

According to Psychology Today, approximately 10% of individuals are effective listeners. Many of us are distracted by background sounds, racing thoughts, our seemingly endless to-do lists, or technology, which makes it more difficult to be a good and active listener. Consequently, we attend to others not necessarily to comprehend them, but to respond. Active listening involves concentrating on what others are saying and engaging them through nonverbal communication. These actions demonstrate your emotional intelligence and aid in the development of your communication abilities.

Try Recording

If you struggle to recognize and comprehend your emotions, it may be a good idea to keep a regular journal. You can use a notebook to reflect on your workday — your meetings, interactions with others, projects, challenges, and successes — and by writing down your thoughts, you will be better able to recognize patterns in your emotions and behavior, as well as your emotional triggers.

Attend Online Classes

Some of us require additional assistance to develop or enhance our emotional intelligence, and this is where online courses and training workshops come in. We have the flexibility to complete coursework at our own pace, network with other professionals, and acquire new knowledge, skills, and insights through courses and workshops. You can also enroll in an online leadership course to supplement your newly acquired emotional intelligence skills.

Chapter 2: How To Complete Employment Application

The job application may request that the tween designate their work availability, including the days and hours they are available to work.

If the adolescent has previous work experience, the job application may request information about their previous positions, including the employer's name, job title, and responsibilities.

Education: The job application may request information about the applicant's education, including their school, grade level, and any pertinent courses or extracurricular activities.

The job application may request that the tween identify relevant skills and abilities, such as computer skills, customer service experience, or knowledge of a specific language or subject.

The application for employment may request the names and contact information for references, such as a teacher or former employer who can attest to the applicant's skills and abilities.

Continuing on

Whenever something substantial is communicated, follow-up can have a significant impact on the difference between success and failure.

Using the above model for layoffs, it will be essential to conduct one more meeting to discuss the subsequent stages with the remaining employees. In addition, it will be necessary to hold meetings in order to ensure that each task performed by those who have been laid off will be completed.

Being Observable

When difficulties become overwhelming, even the most capable leaders must retreat to their office and hide. Nonetheless, being conspicuous is frequently one of the most remarkable forms of administration. Similarly, an entryway strategy in which individuals feel they can approach you with various types of feedback and that these will be taken seriously and treated with deference can be effective.

Developing the Mood

Often, the most important aspect of authority is establishing the atmosphere. A positive, playful leader with a lethal instinct is more likely to gain followers than someone who consistently conveys regrettable messages. In any case, a leader with strong relational skills will want to reevaluate the situation in order to maintain a devoted following when circumstances are dire.

For example, regarding layoffs, it should be clarified that these temporary losses are being made for long-term gains.

In the event that two divisions are merged, a good leader would demonstrate the overall benefits and how the task can be accomplished more efficiently.

Transmitting Change

Many people cannot tolerate change. In spite of the fact that it is an unavoidable reality, people have become so accustomed to their routines that any change can be extremely upsetting and even appear to be a threat to all existence. Having compassion for this perspective can aid in streamlining the changes, despite the fact that it is not usually legitimate.

Organizing Regular Gatherings

Customary gatherings provide an opportunity to communicate clearly and solicit input. Try not to hold gatherings for the sake of holding them. Have distinct meeting objectives, plans, and activity projects at the conclusion of each gathering. Follow up promptly on any activity steps that result from these meetings.

Chapter 3: Why Is Leadership So Indispensable?

Every organization requires effective leadership. Typically, well-led organizations are more productive, competitive, and adaptable to change. Their employees are more engaged and motivated because they have a better grasp of where they are going and why. Long-term profitability tends to increase when an organization is successful at producing leaders.

For the success of your business, you must have strong leaders. Focusing on enhancing and developing leadership skills can enhance the ambiance of the workplace. Organizations require a plan for leadership to ensure that they always have competent and self-confident employees in charge.

development. A strong leadership development strategy may have an impact on the entire organization that transcends the mere presence of a capable leader.

Positive aspects of leadership development

You Can Educate Future Leaders - When a business invests in the development of its workforce, it is investing in the future by identifying individuals who will make outstanding leaders. Leadership development expands the skill sets of current employees, transforming them into the best talent with the potential to have a positive long-term influence on others.

Increases Productivity – With the assistance of a leadership development program, leaders are better equipped to identify issues, generate innovative ideas, and deal with obstacles, all of which can increase the overall productivity of the workforce.

Increased Retention of Top Talent — Employees who are able to acquire new skills and take on new responsibilities can enhance employee loyalty and retention. One of the most common reasons employees abandon a company is poor leadership. A correctly trained leader who provides robust leadership development training for current leaders will increase employee retention.

Helps Facilitate Organizational Changes — Industry shifts are common, and when a great leader is in position, employees are better able to adapt to workplace changes, such as reorganization or new competition.

When executed properly, leadership development can have a significant impact on the profitability of an organization. Improved employee retention can result in greater employee engagement and productivity, as well as have a positive effect on the company's ethos.

Management and training of leadership development can be conducted in a variety of methods. An executive coach can help you get started on the path to developing your leadership skills so that you can have a greater impact on your team and make meaningful changes.

Module 3 Taking personal responsibility

A leader is required to establish and enforce standards. The first area in which you should enforce the standards is on yourself, as your team is looking to you for consistent behavior. Consequently, the ability to set this standard and hold oneself accountable is a crucial aspect of self-leadership. Accountability is now a force from the outside. Accountability occurs when I assign you a task, ensure you complete it, perform as required, and meet the standard, and then penalize you if it is not completed satisfactorily. When we hold ourselves accountable, we don't need someone looking over our shoulders, and we say, "I know this standard, and I will behave in accordance with my own performance standards," and your team is watching you to see if you're responsible, if you hold yourself accountable to the same standards that you hold them to.

What is the difference between leadership responsibility and accountability?

To become a great leader, one must first understand the qualities that distinguish great leaders and the talents that many share. In a remote working environment, the demands placed on leaders have increased while the need for performance persists.

Accountability can take many forms, including objectives, deadlines, and milestones, but at its core, it is simply holding individuals responsible for their actions. This may appear simple and apparent, but in my experience as an entrepreneur and leader, it is frequently the greatest obstacle to achievement.

Why is accountability necessary for a competent leader?

Leadership demands responsibility.

Essentially, it is the act of holding oneself accountable to others. You must be able to hold yourself and those who report to you accountable for your actions and decisions in order to be an effective leader.

People who lack a sense of accountability will not accept personal responsibility for themselves, nor will they be held accountable by colleagues or management for their own or other team members' actions.

It is founded on hypotheses. It is essential to be transparent with all parties involved regarding what you anticipate and why. People take responsibility for their actions when they feel accountable for them and when they can readily rectify any errors.

Three Ways to Demonstrate and Instill Leadership Accountability

Accountable leaders and their teams model a variety of behaviors in the service of fostering a higher-performing culture.

1. Transmission

Your team must be able to communicate effectively if they are to achieve purpose alignment and clarity. People must have faith that their leaders can provide unambiguous direction. When there is ambiguity in communication, teams lose focus and become disengaged.

Are the expectations of your team crystal clear?

If you ask someone to do something and they do not, it is possible that they did not hear or comprehend your request, or that they were preoccupied with something else. This can result in confusion and frustration, both of which are detrimental to your efforts' success.

Creating feedback opportunities within your team is an excellent method to determine where communication is failing and how to improve it.

The most effective mode of communication must be considered by leaders of remote teams. Any technological tools must support accountability by monitoring the alignment of focus areas and duties.

Creating opportunities for your team to share an experience, get to know one another, and develop a sense of camaraderie and collaboration is essential for building trust in this environment.

Delegation 2.

Even virtually hovering over an employee's shoulder is ineffective for fostering a strong, accountable team culture.

Focus on being organized and helping your team comprehend their focus areas and how you can assist them in achieving their objectives.

When individuals feel accountable for their actions, they take ownership of them and are able to swiftly correct any errors. This increases the level of trust between leaders and their teams.

Make your team members feel accountable for their actions if you want to be an effective leader. Focus on holding the team to the same standards that you would, and keep them invested in the team's shared objective.

3. Listening

Whether remote-first or office-first, listening paths are now an essential component of effective leadership.

Creating an environment in which your team is heard, areas of concern are communicated, and growth opportunities are pursued is a crucial aspect of fostering an accountability culture. Teams prefer leaders who empower others and cultivate an environment of openness over those who exercise authoritative or consultative leadership.

Greater emphasis must be placed on demonstrating that you are a supportive and compassionate leader. Closely following this is employee-centricity, which must commence with listening.

Chapter 4: Leadership Qualities To Adopt

When we consider the fundamental characteristics of a leader, we typically receive as many responses as individuals we consult. However, there are a few characteristics on which nearly everyone agrees. In this section, we will examine some of these characteristics.

Communication

This cannot be conveyed sufficiently. Good leaders are excellent communicators. There are two primary aspects of communication: the ability to be clear and empathetic in dialogues with others, and the ability to listen with an open mind and open heart. It is essential to master both verbal and written communication within organizations. As the world becomes flooded with emails and instant communications on a variety of platforms, it becomes more difficult to always communicate with respect and intention. Therefore, it is a leader's responsibility to use diverse platforms so as not to confuse their followers. Also, communication that causes excessive distress should be eliminated. Always strive to keep your messages brief, concise, and full of pertinent information.

When it comes to listening to your employees, it is essential to solicit feedback on a regular basis. Demonstrate that you are receptive to constructive criticism and attentive to their concerns without taking offense. This requires effort. You cannot initially expect your people to come to you with their problems because they may not trust you to comprehend them. However, you may find it simpler to connect with them as time passes. To acquire the trust of your team and set the tone for them, you should avoid gossip at all costs. When you demonstrate to your team that you respect their boundaries and do not judge them unnecessarily, you will cultivate an environment where everyone communicates with empathy.

The final aspect of communication involves dependability. First, you must ensure that your communication aligns with the larger visions and objectives of your organization and team. This implies that you should maintain a consistent tone throughout. Second, you must ensure that whatever you communicate to your team is carried out. Do not make false promises, overcommit, or neglect to follow through on your commitments. At all times, let your actions validate what you say.

Vision Leaders have distinct visions for their respective organizations. You cannot effectively guide your people if you do not know where you are leading them, right? When setting objectives for your team, be sure to consider their unique perspectives. Only when everyone is in agreement with your objective will they make an effort to accomplish it. Everything you do (or don't do) should be done with the team's overarching vision in mind.

Accepting and embracing change is an essential aspect of having and attaining a vision. You are responsible for convincing your team of the positive aspects of change, as it is inevitable that it will make them restless. Your organization's vision should not be rigid; rather, it should be fluid and adaptable. You must also set an example for your team by demonstrating how change can benefit their individual career development.

Critical Reasoning

Critical thinking is a skill that all individuals should possess. This is effective on multiple levels. To be a critical thinker, you must first ensure that you are receiving sufficient information from relevant sources. You cannot make decisions with contaminated or insufficient information. Currently, the issue is that we receive far too much information. Therefore, the challenge is to determine which data are trustworthy and beneficial.

The second component of critical thinking is the formulation of a problem statement. A thorough problem statement makes it much simpler to find a solution that works for all parties. Once you have a clear understanding of the problem, you can move on to the third step, which requires you to identify its fundamental causes.

When examining the causes of a problem, we are prone to accept the first item that comes to mind. This is not to say that it could not be a cause, but it is not sufficient to address the issue. It is more accurately a symptom than a cause. When we continue to pose pertinent questions, we will eventually arrive at the root causes of our problems. This brings us to the fourth aspect of critical thinking, which is coming up with original solutions to problems. Again, these solutions should be the consequence of team brainstorming.

Critical thinkers are also aware that a solution is incomplete without a feedback cycle. This is the final step of the problem-solving procedure, during which you ensure that your solution is implemented in real time and that any issues are resolved in a timely manner. Your approach to problems enables your team to learn and develop their own problem-solving routines.

Accountability

This is possibly the most difficult trait to acquire. When in a position of authority, we may be tempted to abdicate responsibility for our actions. It is challenging to always hold ourselves and others accountable. Accountability involves not only recognizing our errors, but also taking the necessary steps to correct them. It is essential to identify and communicate to our teams the consequences of our actions.

By holding ourselves and others accountable, we foster an environment of trust and openness. Our people are aware that we adhere to the same standards as they do. They can come to us with any problem, even if we are the cause of the problem. Most importantly, we demonstrate the significance of leadership accountability.

Additionally, a sense of stability results from this. When employees recognize that their leaders are dependable and accountable, they feel more confident. They do not anticipate unpleasant circumstances or misplaced consequences, nor do they anticipate being held accountable for someone else's errors. In this way, everyone accepts responsibility for their actions and does their absolute best.

Empathy

A compassionate leader sets the tone for a compassionate workplace. Empathy and compassion have always been essential components of successful organizations, but in recent years they have become unquestionably indispensable. Leaders who lack empathy risk alienating their employees and, in the long run, even losing them. Without empathy, your employees may feel inconsequential. They begin to believe in themselves and feel connected to their work when they are treated with empathy. It also inspires optimism for their future within and beyond the organization. While it is true that some individuals are naturally more sensitive and empathetic than others, everyone can become more empathetic through practice.

The most essential task is to cultivate meaningful relationships with your employees. This involves taking a genuine interest in their lives while maintaining professional boundaries. You must ascertain their level of confidence prior to informing them that they can come to you with any issues that interfere with their concentration and performance at work. Obviously, it is also essential to reassure them that they will not be punished for being honest about their struggles.

Additionally, you should make an effort to become acquainted with the interests, activities, and aspirations of your team members. In this way, you will not only be able to appreciate them for who they are as a whole, but you will also be able to assist them in utilizing their strengths to improve their employment. You can also help them celebrate significant personal achievements and provide support when they are struggling with personal issues. When in doubt, ask queries to better comprehend the situation. Always opt for curiosity over judgment.

Currently, signs of burnout are the most essential things to be on the lookout for.

Traditionally, exhaustion affects those who work in professions involving caregiving, such as healthcare. It is now significantly more prevalent among all types of employees. When an employee is experiencing burnout, they feel so fatigued that they become disengaged from their work and environment. They may even lack motivation to perform. Undiagnosed or untreated burnout can contribute to serious conditions such as depression.

Your employees may experience burnout for a variety of reasons, including a lack of appreciation and support, hostile working conditions, and unremitting stress. Frequently, employees don't realize they're on the verge of exhaustion until it's too late, which is why it's crucial to check in with them frequently. Check for signs of exhaustion and ask if there is anything you can do to improve their situation.

Even if you are unable to provide tangible assistance, merely listening to them with empathy can make them feel supported.

It is commonly said that to cultivate empathy, one must walk a mile in another person's shoes. Although this is an effective means to comprehend how others feel, it is not always possible. Sometimes, we simply lack the necessary experiences to identify with others. What should we do in this situation? Well, we let the people speak for themselves, and when they share their experiences, we believe them. Sometimes, centering the experiences of others in a narrative can be the most empathic act, and genuine leaders endeavor to do so frequently.

Gratitude

Gratitude enhances our appreciation for what we already possess and prepares us for future success. The majority of people become agitated and angry when faced with adversity. Others buckle under duress, with their teams frequently bearing the brunt of their actions. Even when things are going well, some supervisors have difficulty expressing appreciation to their team members. This impacts morale and decreases people's confidence in their ability to perform well.

When you express gratitude to your team and encourage them to cultivate an attitude of gratitude, you increase their commitment to their employment. In addition, they feel more connected to their colleagues in the workplace. As daily interactions become more optimistic and positive, individuals feel that their contributions are significant. Furthermore, when your team encounters a difficulty, they do not yield up. Therefore, gratitude fosters resilience, which is a crucial success factor.

You can cultivate gratitude in yourself and your team members through simple acts such as celebrating minor victories, regularly complimenting your employees on their work, and publicly and privately thanking them for their contributions. A decent rule of thumb is to praise in public and criticize in private. Thus, your team will always be aware of your commitment to their development and well-being. Humility is another trait that can facilitate gratitude. A great leader is always modest. In actuality, they attribute their successes to their teammates and accept responsibility for their failures.

Chapter 5: The key to success is team cohesion and collaboration.

At one point or another, we have all participated in a group endeavor. Some of these groups may have been enjoyable, effective, and potent, while others were distressing, ineffective, and burdensome. While many groups function admirably together, only a cohesive group makes genuine advancement. Expanded group attachment in the workplace has led to increased achievement, job satisfaction, colleague confidence, and decreased tension.

Being a cohesive group entails not only achieving the group's objectives, but also having everyone feel as though they contributed to the group's overall success. Individuals in a cohesive group are typically more motivated to pursue the group objective than their own interests.

Productivity and success are more likely to occur when team members are aligned and working towards the same objectives, and when there is a positive and supportive team culture.

The following are strategies for promoting team cohesion and collaboration:

Establish clear goals and objectives: Establishing clear goals and objectives ensures that everyone is on the same page and working toward the same end result.

Encourage open communication: Encourage open and honest communication between team members, and solicit their feedback and suggestions. This can aid in fostering collaboration and establishing trust.

Encourage team members to collaborate and provide mutual support, and recognize and reward collaboration.

A positive team culture is necessary for nurturing collaboration and cohesion. Encourage a culture of respect, support, and inclusiveness, and establish a setting where team members feel comfortable and valued.

Listed below are some additional applications of team cohesion and collaboration:

When team members can collaborate and exchange ideas, they are more likely to generate creative and effective solutions to problems.

When team members are able to collaborate effectively, tasks are more likely to be accomplished efficiently and on schedule.

By promoting open communication and collaboration, you can leverage the collective knowledge and expertise of your team to identify and solve problems more efficiently.

A positive team culture and strong team cohesion can result in increased job satisfaction and enhanced team morale.

Overall, team cohesion and collaboration are crucial to the success of any endeavor or undertaking. By cultivating these traits, you will be better equipped to face future challenges and achieve your objectives.

Chapter 6: Types Of Leadership

Listed below are various forms of leadership that reflect some of the power discussed previously:

a) The Charismatic Leader - This form of leader's influence is primarily derived from his personal qualities. The only issue is that not everyone possesses exceptional qualities that can inspire others to pursue them. Moreover, these characteristics cannot be acquired through formal education. The charismatic leaders Jesus Christ, Napoleon, and Winston Churchill are examples. A charismatic manager will undoubtedly have a significant impact on others and subordinates.

b) The Situation Leader - This is a transitory form of leadership whose effectiveness depends on the leader's presence at the appropriate time and place. This type of leadership is inappropriate for an individual concern due to its transient nature, as what is required is a leader who can perform a leadership role in various situations for an extended period.

c) The Traditional Leader - This is an inherited position, as leadership is a matter of birth. For instance, kingship or queenship is a position conferred by birth into a regal family, making it impossible for many individuals to aspire to.

d) The Appointed Leader - The position held grants this individual leadership responsibilities. In other words, this type of leader's legitimate power derives from his formal authority within the hierarchy.

e) The Functional Leader - For this type of leader, what he does rather than who he is determines his leadership position. For instance, a leader's effectiveness is contingent on his ability to meet task, group, and individual requirements. He can meet task requirements by assigning responsibilities and establishing performance standards, or he can fulfill group requirements by functioning as a representative. On an individual level, he may choose to counsel or inspire people.

Outstanding historical leaders

It can be beneficial to recall the famous leaders of the past. There are numerous biographies devoted to these luminaries.

The best leaders of history were fascinating and influential:

Winston Churchill was a world leader. Churchill, the British prime minister during World War II, was renowned for his efforts to incite resistance against Nazi Germany. He was able to thrive under challenging circumstances and exhibited tremendous determination and commitment.

- Churchill is widely regarded as the foremost leader of the 20th century.

Franklin D. Roosevelt. Roosevelt overcame polio and limb paralysis to become president of the United States four times. Roosevelt lead the nation through the Great Depression and World War II with success.

King, Martin Luther, Jr. Have you ever desired to transform society? Martin Luther King Jr. is regarded as the nation's foremost civil rights leader. Courage, perseverance, and a nonviolent stance were his defining characteristics. He even won the Nobel Prize.

Abraham Lincoln. Lincoln was able to lead the United States through the Civil War and initiate the North-South unification process. Lincoln was renowned for his modesty and resolve. Lincoln is considered by many historians to be the finest U.S. president.

Mahatma Gandhi. Gandhi was successful in removing the British from India without resorting to violence. Gandhi, a common citizen, was able to inspire a country to engage in sufficient civil disobedience to secure India's independence from British rule.

Gandhi is regarded by many as the greatest leader in human history.

Adolph Hitler, Genghis Khan. Not all influential leaders are remembered favorably. Hitler and Genghis Khan are examples of such individuals. They were effective at leading a large number of people, even if you disapproved of what they stood for.

Not all great leaders are also wonderful individuals. However, all exceptional leaders possess the capacity to motivate and influence others. There is much to be learned from the past's famous leaders. Utilize this information and reap the benefits.

Chapter 7: Leadership Variations
Administrative Authority

Authoritarian leadership styles permit the imposition of expectations and the definition of outcomes. In situations where a leader is the most knowledgeable member of the team, a one-person performance can be successful. Although this is a time-efficient strategy, creativity will be sacrificed due to the limited participation of the team. When team members require precise directives, the authoritarian leadership style is also used.

Time spent on making critical decisions can be shortened. The chain of command can be emphasized explicitly. Errors in the execution of plans can be minimized.

The use of an authoritative leadership style produces consistent outcomes.

A very rigorous leadership style can occasionally result in employee rebellion.

It stifles employee innovation and creativity.

It diminishes group cohesion and collaboration.

Group participation is drastically reduced.

Leadership that is authoritarian increases employee turnover.

Participative Administration

The democratic theory is the foundation of participative leadership approaches. Involving team members in the decision-making process is essential. Thus, team members experience inclusion, engagement, and motivation to contribute. Typically, the supervisor will have the final say in decision-making processes. However, if there are disagreements within a group, reaching consensus can be a time-consuming process.

It increases motivation and employment satisfaction among employees. It encourages employees to use their creativity.

A participative leadership style contributes to the formation of an effective team.

A high level of productivity is attainable.

The decision-making process becomes more time-consuming.

There is a high likelihood that leaders will apologize to employees.

Communication failures can sometimes arise. Transparency in information sharing can lead to security problems.

If the employees are inexperienced, poor decisions may be made.

Delegative administration

A delegative leadership style, also known as "laissez-faire leadership", emphasizes delegating initiative to team members. This can be an effective strategy if team members are competent, willing to assume responsibility, and prefer individual work. However, disagreements among members can cause a group to fragment and lose motivation and morale.

Chapter 8: Communication

Communication is the demonstration or interaction of utilizing words, sounds, signs, or methods of behaving to communicate or exchange information or to communicate one's thoughts, considerations, emotions, etc. to another individual.

No matter how you look at it, it is one of the most important communication skills that we must all develop and hone throughout our careers. "Communicating information and ideas" is consistently regarded as one of the most important skills for achieving long-term success. Communication is also embedded in a variety of other leadership abilities and skills, such as "driving representatives," "participative leadership," and "building and patching connections."

Without exceptional communication skills, it is extremely difficult to become an exceptional leader. I want to believe that you noticed that the preceding sentence did not imply that you are an exceptional communicator - the contrast is striking. Infrequently can the path to becoming a gifted communicator be found in the academic sphere. From our earliest days in the homeroom, we are prepared to focus on articulation, vernacular, presence, conveyance, punctuation, and so on.

We are instructed to focus on ourselves at the close of each day. Leaders urgently need to learn the more unpretentious elements of correspondence (elements that emphasize others) that are rarely emphasized in the classroom. In the following section, I'll discuss a few communication traits that, when utilized consistently, will assist you in achieving more effective communication outcomes.

Communication precedes leadership. Successful communication is unambiguous, direct, and tailored to the recipient. A good leader will have some leeway in determining which communication manner and method (message, email, phone, or face-to-face) works best for each team member. You build trust, compatibility, and a culture of shared responsibility by communicating with your group. Frequent, clear, and sincere communication.

Effective communication is essential for establishing trust, adjusting efforts in pursuit of goals, and bringing about positive change. When there is a lack of communication, vital information can be misunderstood, resulting in connections that persist and, ultimately, obstacles that impede progress.

If you're interested in enhancing your leadership abilities, here are eight relational skills that will make you a more effective employee. essential abilities of compelling communicator:

1. Sympathy

Sympathy. The capacity to experience and think as another. The highest level of reception. You must not only listen to a person's words, but also comprehend how they feel.

In terms of leadership, empathy isn't just a nice-to-have; it's essential for establishing trust, certainty, and commitment within your team.

The capacity to comprehend and relate to the thoughts and experiences of others is empathy. Leaders who operate from a place of compassion, understanding, and empathy establish more stable relationships among their subordinates and enhance execution in all circumstances.

2. Absolute concentration

Leaders with persuasive influence know when to speak and, more importantly, when to listen. Request the viewpoints, opinions, and criticism of your employees to demonstrate that you care. Moreover, when they do share, effectively contribute to the discussion by suggesting conversation initiates, encouraging them to elaborate, and taking notes.

It is necessary to maintain silence and avoid intervening. Maintain your attention on the representative and what they are saying. In addition, you must eliminate any distractions, such as your wireless's persistent alerts or the display of incoming messages.

3. straight-forwardness

By communicating openly about the organization's goals, great opportunities, and challenges, leaders can build trust among their group and foster an environment in which employees feel encouraged to share their ideas and work together. Recognizing errors empowers trial and error and creates a safe haven for dynamic critical thinking.

Each individual should recognize the contribution they make to the success of the organization. Representatives find it simpler to follow leaders who are more forthright.

4. Lucidity

Particulars should be discussed with representatives. Define the ideal outcome of a project or major initiative, and be explicit about what you expect to see at the conclusion of each accomplishment. If goals are not being met, consider refining your message or asking how you can provide additional clarity or assistance.

Less confusion will be associated with your needs the more lucid you are. Representatives will comprehend what they are pursuing and consequently feel more engaged.

5. Open non-verbal communication

Focus on your non-verbal communication to ensure that you are conveying the intended message. If you are attempting to rouse someone, speaking with clenched fists and a furrowed brow will not send the appropriate message. Engage visually to demonstrate interest and compatibility, and emit a genuine smile to convey affection and trust, all other factors being equal.

How can leaders build trust in Communication? Through consistency. Verbalize whatever it is that you will incessantly bring about. Ensure your messages are consistent with what you say and how you behave. Continually, as if by routine. Demonstrating your solidity and dependability to your employees is a fundamental and effective method for establishing trust.

▪ Character. Being a considerate person who makes the best choice. Be accountable and acknowledge errors. Your representatives will adhere to this pattern once you have demonstrated how to do something.

▪ Lucidity. In any correspondence with representatives, you should be explicit and concise when discussing strategies and objectives. Always be realistic, and never make promises that you cannot keep.

⁃ Efforts coordinated. Asking for employee input demonstrates that you value the opinions and criticisms of others. By remembering them for the interaction, but using their ideas, you build trust and loyalty over the long term while incorporating them into the agreement.

⁃ Mindful. Deny discussed the importance of compassion and empathic receptivity in the video. Recognize the feelings and concerns of others to demonstrate your concern.

Chapter 9: Balance And The Importance Of Self-Care

We can have a successful family and career simultaneously. To achieve this, however, we must be able to take time for ourselves and prioritize our health. This is the only way we will have sufficient time and energy to care for everyone and everything.

If we don't place ourselves first, we will lose everything we've poured so much sweat, blood, and tears into constructing. This was undoubtedly the case with a close friend who launched a phenomenal catering business that was an instant success. Like many women, she desired to assist as many people as possible, participate in her community, and provide for her family. She had not yet learned how to say no and when to assert her boundaries. Numerous individuals calling for additional assistance or favors caused her phone to vibrate nonstop. On the weekends, she spent the entire day managing orders and attempting to satisfy insane last-minute requests. She never had time for herself, and her lack of boundaries began to negatively impact her career and personal life. However, she continued to overextend herself, giving too much of herself without ever saying "no." She eventually wound up in the hospital with a variety of issues that could have been avoided if she had learned to take better care of herself and balance her priorities.

There is a limit to a person's endurance before they become exhausted. Yes, I am aware that renowned leaders make balancing work and family appear effortless. This frequently makes us feel terrible when we are experiencing difficulty. We believe that we are doing something incorrectly. Always keep in mind that there will be obstacles, regardless of who you are. When asked how she managed the work-life balance, Reese Witherspoon responded, "I'm just holding on, trying to make it through."

You too can persevere if you believe in your role as a leader and keep in mind that you are setting an example for your children and other women who will inspire them and fuel their own passion.

Chapter 10: Qualities Of Leadership

Diligence
This requires deploying all necessary resources to ensure the completion of the task. Here, the leader will focus his time and effort on establishing an example for the followers. Because planning is a continuous process, it is essential to involve stakeholders at each stage of decision-making. Work ethic transforms obstacles into opportunities for achieving group, organizational, or personal objectives.

Equitability
This enables consistency in relationships with others, especially when subordinates are at fault. A leader is considered fair when he listens to all aspects of a story before rendering a verdict. Here, the decision is founded on the received data. In this endeavor, the

leader must be able to handle each follower equally, irrespective of their relationship to him or her. This has the effect of rewarding the leader for the followers' loyalty and commitment to the group's objective or direction.

Self-effacement

Humility emphasizes that a leader is in their position not because they are superior to their adherents, but to serve and provide guidance. Here, they will not exalt themselves or place themselves above others, but rather seek means to elevate others.

This has the effect of placing all followers at ease; if so, it is self-motivating and followers will be more loyal to the leader.

Confidence

It is the leader's ability to communicate his expectations clearly in order to avoid future conflicts. In this section, the leader will articulate his life's ambitions.

However, it is the leader's responsibility to comprehend the ramifications of their decisions and expectations, as well as any potential threats to their positions. However, this must be done in moderation, as excessive assertiveness could be interpreted as aggression and insufficient assertiveness would be detrimental to completing the task.

Inventive

As a leader, you should possess creative qualities, as people frequently expect you to be innovative. Even if you are not very problem-oriented, thinking creatively ensures that you will not be limited in your solution options. You are guaranteed to investigate issues in ways that others may not have considered. If you consider all possible outcomes, this will appear extreme in the majority of cases.

Contrary to the old belief that better methods of doing things are desirable, the majority of organizations, groups, and individuals must be creative today. This should ideally bring out everyone's creative side, which can sometimes lead to novel solutions and ideas. Thinking creatively means approaching problems, situations, projects, and any endeavor requiring a detailed thought process with an open mind and in novel and inventive ways.

Exploring the various options available would enable the implementation of methods that are potentially more energy-, time-, and resource-efficient, and therefore have a chance of being adopted. Occasionally, borrowing methods from completely unrelated platforms and adapting them to an individual's current requirements can yield surprising and intriguing results. Also utilizing best practices, but adding or modifying certain areas, can produce remarkable outcomes. In addition, another method to practice lateral thinking is by soliciting advice from sources that would ordinarily appear absurd.

Encouraging people to express their point of view without imposing restrictions on their creativity, attempting new methods or copying other successful formulas, but also adding a personal touch, demonstrates an innovative spirit. Inviting and evaluating random applications can also revitalize a business or project that has become stagnant or monotonous.

It is sometimes beneficial to take a step back and examine the situation from a completely foreign perspective and thought process in order to redefine the processes currently used to introduce newer and riskier applications that can breathe new life into the situation.

Wit

Even when discussing the most fundamental topics, there is always an element of tension, regardless of how close the followers are to the leader. You can always strengthen your relationship with your followers by incorporating humor. This breaks the frost and invigorates your followers. As a result, you have a great deal more control over the group, as members can identify with you.

However, it is essential to limit the amount of levity in your speech. Ensure that the humor you use will not offend anyone. Because it is likely to offend someone, humor that comments on a person's culture or physical anatomy is undesirable in the group. In this context, it is essential that you impart philanthropic intelligence and wisdom.

Foresightedness

A leader must have a distinct understanding of the destination of their organization, team, or group. At all times, the course of action is determined by the organization's vision. Here, only the processes are altered, not the organization's vision. As a leader, you must coordinate resources and processes in order to achieve the primary objective. You must frequently refer to the organization's or group's vision because it serves as the foundation of your leadership. People decide whether they want to identify with you or with the group based on the group's perspective. People will only identify with the group if their objectives align with those of the organization.

Chapter 11: Some Qualities Of A Genuine Leader

Here are eight characteristics of a genuine leader, along with advice on how to exhibit them in the workplace:

demonstrates integrity

A genuine leader acts with integrity, which entails adhering to ethical principles in all aspects of life. They should communicate these values at work to provide a foundation for the employee conduct they expect. Integrity will assist you in gaining respect, which will inspire your team to follow your leadership. Integrity also establishes your credibility in the workplace, as employees will feel they can rely on you to make morally sound decisions in all situations.

To demonstrate your integrity at work, you should set a good example for your colleagues. For instance, always adhere to organizational policies and respect others. Demonstrate to your employees that you are committed to producing high-quality work and maintaining a good reputation, and they should do the same.

2. Helps others to grow

A genuine leader should seek to maximize the potential of their team members. By assisting team members in developing their abilities, they increase the team's potential and, as a result, benefit the entire organization. Employees desire career advancement; therefore, they will be more receptive to a leader who provides opportunities for growth.

One way to develop employees is by delegating tasks; these are duties that the leader can perform themselves, but which provide the assigned employees with an opportunity to learn something new or hone specific skills. You will also benefit because you will have more time to focus on important or time-consuming tasks. When attempting to develop your team, be sure to allow individuals to make their own decisions. You must establish boundaries and guidelines, but giving employees more decision-making power will help them advance and feel more fulfilled in their duties.

esteems partnerships

A genuine leader should prioritize their relationships with team members over their status as a leader. To achieve this, leaders should collaborate with their team members rather than designating them tasks alone. They should take the time to get to know each member as an individual and develop more personal relationships with them. When members of your team feel valued on an individual level, they will be more motivated because they know their efforts are valued.

Thanking your team members or expressing gratitude in other ways after they have completed duties is a simple way to demonstrate your appreciation for them. Delivering encouraging communications is another straightforward method of expressing gratitude. For instance, if you believed an employee did an excellent job during a presentation to a client, you should let them know afterward. When employees are confident that they are performing well at work, they can improve their performance even further.

4. Accepts personal accountability

A genuine leader must accept responsibility for their actions and demand the same of their subordinates. They should hold themselves to a high standard of work, thereby serving as a model for others. Accountability entails acknowledging one's errors and demonstrating professional methods of recovery. Creating an environment where accountability is valued can increase team members' performance and trust because it demonstrates that they can rely on one another to carry out their responsibilities.

One method for implementing accountability in the workplace is to provide specific feedback on substandard work. Ensure direct and respectful communication with individuals in order to assist them in understanding their errors and how to correct them. Similarly, you should commend team members who demonstrate signs of improvement. Employees will be more motivated to adhere to your high standards if they feel respected and observe you adhering to these standards in your own work.

5. Displays honesty

A genuine leader is always willing to engage their employees in candid and open dialogue. Being trustworthy creates a sense of respect and a propensity to follow your lead among team members. When you take the time to communicate with your employees and tell them the truth, they feel valued. Ensure that you communicate frequently with your team, as this will help everyone feel more at ease with candid conversations.

To demonstrate honesty, provide your employees with the necessary information explicitly. For instance, you should be transparent with your team about any organizational changes and how they may affect them. You can also demonstrate honesty on a daily basis by providing feedback to your team members and, if possible, hosting regular check-ins.

6. Engages in attentive attention

A genuine leader should always listen to both positive and negative employee feedback. They should allow workers to express their opinions without interrupting or evaluating them. A good listener also strives to comprehend and empathize with the speaker's thoughts and emotions.

Make it plain to your employees that you are available to hear their questions, concerns, ideas, and suggestions, which will help them feel valued at work and more involved with the team. Maintain eye contact and ask clarifying questions to demonstrate that you are engaged and listening during these conversations.

A true leader employs a vision, whether it is their own or that of the company, to motivate and inspire their employees to achieve their goals. By communicating their vision to the team, the leader fosters a shared sense of purpose that provides members with direction and motivation. A true leader has the ability to persuade others to support their vision, whether by making it pertinent to employees or by presenting a story that helps them visualize the outcome.

Always communicate your clearly-defined vision to your team and assist them in comprehending how their responsibilities support that vision. Employees will feel empowered when they understand how they can contribute to the success of the team. Assist your team in maintaining focus by designating project-wide objectives and explaining how their accomplishment advances the vision. Provide feedback and encouragement when individuals achieve these objectives.

8. Exhibits fortitude

A true leader is fearless in the face of potential conflict or criticism, particularly when they are confident that their actions are for the team's benefit. Employees revere a leader who advocates for their best interests in all circumstances. Possessing a strong set of values and a clear vision enables a true leader to face any challenge with fortitude.

In addition to displaying confidence in your decisions and confronting conflicts, being courageous at work may also involve the ability to be straightforward with your employees. Being a leader entails making decisions that have a direct impact on your team members, so it is essential to act with confidence and bravery.

Chapter 12: Adapting To Change: The Importance Of Assessing And Modifying Your Objectives

Setting objectives can be an effective means of concentrating your efforts and boosting your motivation. When you establish a goal, you give yourself something specific to work towards, which can keep you motivated and on course. To ensure that your objectives remain pertinent and attainable, you must, however, periodically assess and modify them as necessary.

The ability to adapt to changing circumstances or new information is one of the benefits of reviewing and modifying your objectives. For instance, if you established a goal based on incorrect assumptions, you may need to revise it in light of the new information. This can assist you in remaining focused on your goals and making progress toward attaining them.

Additionally, reviewing and revising your objectives can keep you motivated and on track. By regularly reviewing your objectives, you can identify any potential difficulties or obstacles that might be impeding your success. This can increase the likelihood of achieving your objectives by keeping you motivated and focused.

In conclusion, establishing goals can be an effective method for concentrating efforts and boosting motivation. To ensure that your objectives remain pertinent and attainable, you must, however, periodically assess and modify them as necessary. By routinely reviewing and adjusting your goals, you can better adapt to changing conditions and maintain focus on your long-term objectives.

A fearless commander standing before his wing-like representation.

Fearlessness is abundant among genuine leaders; consequently, they are acquainted with their skills and leadership qualities. They are confident in their skills and leadership qualities. They have a healthy sense of identity and self-assurance, and they acknowledge that they can have an effect. You must have confidence in your abilities and be sufficiently tenacious to complete all tasks. Fearlessness is essential for leadership because it enables individuals to confront obstacles, accomplish goals, and soar to great heights. Hierarchical leaders assume personal responsibility and walk with confidence. It enables them to make fast decisions and deal with hierarchical issues and conflicts. Great leaders take full responsibility and act swiftly, without transferring the buck, overlooking, or hesitating.

6. Visionary

A faraway visionary leader using a hand-held telescope

A visionary leader is far-sighted and motivated by the potential of an organization. Visionary leaders exert great effort for the benefit of all and maintain their own vitality through time and change. A visionary leader ensures an ideal for the future with consistency and ensures that everyone contributes to the cycle.

A visionary leader is not timid in the face of difficulties and eccentric decisions.

Effective Communicator

A supervisor communicating with its colleague

Incredible correspondence is the path to leadership success. A successful leader knows how to effectively communicate his message. They are excellent communicators who help the recipient complete his or her task. They choose terms and expressions that are appropriate to the situation and allow others to express their perspectives and thoughts. They are aware of how crucial it is to have excellent interpersonal skills. They are extremely perceptive and learn from the behavior of others, which provides them with a profound understanding of human complexities.

Designation

A leader designating elite individuals on a whiteboard.

The ability to delegate is an excellent leadership quality. A good leader who knows how to delegate wisely and maximize the results. Designation is essential for enhancing efficiency and group performance. Similarly, a leader is the most prominent member of any organization. Therefore, knowing when and how to appoint provides them with additional opportunities to focus on their most important tasks. Moreover, it is crucial to note that the ability to delegate is not limited to assigning tasks to others. Additionally, it requires the awareness and comprehension of who possesses the necessary skills and mastery to complete the task. To save time and future burdens, meticulous assignment is essential.

9. Thinking capacity

A leader selecting two strategies

Great executives are decisive and understand how to assist the organization, its representatives, partners, and clients. You could never conceive of a leader who is vague and dubious. Great executives are cognizant of the fact that their decisions can determine the fate of an organization. They evaluate a situation multiple times before reaching a conclusion. Prior to making declarations, they collect the required essential data. Similarly, prior to making a decision, they conduct their own investigation into what is occurring or the nature of the problem.

10. Skills in critical reasoning

Good leaders are critical thinkers by nature.

Leadership positions are not limited to administrators and appointing. Today's business executives have an expanded range of leadership responsibilities. For an organization to function properly, its executives must be able to think critically and examine what is occurring in order to make better decisions.

Critical thought skills are indispensable for effective leadership.

Great leaders have the innate ability to solve problems. They are equipped with the ability to identify and classify issues. Investigate, utilize, and communicate in order to resolve the issues.

Improving one's critical thinking skills is essential for any leader who wishes to eliminate obstacles.

11. Fair Attitude

A leader with a reasonable demeanor - advancing representatives in anticipation of their execution

We as a group have distinct dispositions. Those who can consider and act beyond this circle distinguish themselves from the group. These tendencies are one of the reasons why most leaders fail to attain more prominent positions.

Great leaders are considerate of the employees and the cycles of the organization. They consistently account for the well-being of all individuals and celebrate excellence.

They recognize that nothing significant has ever been accomplished with an unreasonable and one-sided mindset. Regardless of the case, the result's supportability is consistently dubious.

Great leaders throw prejudice and injustice out the window and create a culture that does not promote or acknowledge this disposition.

12. Curiosity

A-curious leader observing the elite of realities through a magnifying lens on a white screen.

Have you ever viewed extraordinary leaders sharing their stories and experiences in Ted-talks? I presume you have. If you haven't already, I suggest you do so immediately.

You would acknowledge these leaders' intelligence and curiosity. In addition, their consistent willingness to learn new things. Their considerations, thoughts, and insights are unique and provocative. This is due to their natural curiosity and interest in life. They pursue various interests and continue to invest resources in it. They are open to expanding their offerings through craft, innovation, and science. Additionally, all the world's capability. This trait enables them to develop a rational and inspiring perspective on all issues.

13. Self-propelled

A self-motivated leader who scribbles "I can't, I won't" on a wall.

The ability to persuade others is one of the fundamental characteristics of effective leaders. When necessary, great leaders rouse and energize their employees. Even in dangerous conditions, they navigate their canoe without incident. They maintain their own motivation and set an example for others to follow.

14. Modesty

Modesty toward others is a foundational trait of a moral leader.

The greatest leaders are the most modest ones. This assertion is not one that I assert to be true. When we consider leadership, modesty is not the quality that immediately comes to mind. However, it is one of the essential qualities of a good leader. It is for this reason that modesty is frequently overshadowed by the ostentatiousness of the lauded leadership qualities.

Unafraid and resolute leaders comprehend the connection between leadership and serving the common good. They result in change, not devastation. They are aware of their strengths and weaknesses and consistently desire to grow and provide more.

Regard for Others

Great leaders maintain a healthy work-life balance. Good leaders recognize the significance of work-life balance. They recognize that the wellbeing and health of individuals within the organization play a significant role in attaining success.

They motivate their coworkers and guarantee that the staff, clients, recipients, and clients feel trusted.

They understand the importance of appreciating and recognizing employees, as well as fostering mutual respect and understanding within the organization.

They make progress toward creating an environment where everyone can flourish.

16. Self-control

Great leaders are self-controlled and have excellent time management skills.

Exceptional leadership entails instilling discipline in others. Great leaders are self-controlled and have excellent time management skills. They invigorate a culture in which individuals are centered. This is the capacity for individuals to consistently adapt. When you are self-taught and set an example, you inspire others to follow.

In an organization where time is of the essence and employees are overburdened with responsibilities, being more focused can help employees accomplish more and keep the office peaceful.

17. The capacity to comprehend people at their essence

A-inwardly Intelligent leader deliberating and taking decisive action

Recognizing, adapting to, evaluating, and understanding one's own emotions and those of those around us constitutes the capacity to deeply appreciate others.

Five components comprise the capacity to comprehend individuals at their core:

Mindfulness

Self-guideline

Compassion Inspiration and Interpersonal Skills

Great leaders are mindful, take command, and make decisive decisions without losing control. They understand the perspectives of others without being pessimistic. They are self-motivated and have strong interpersonal skills, which aid them in forming associations and secure connections. These indicate that exceptional leaders possess a high degree of Emotional Intelligence. To this end, the ability to comprehend anyone on a deep level is one of the most essential leadership qualities.

18. Energy

Leaders are enthusiastic about their objectives and objectives.

Energy is a common leadership trait observed in the world's most effective leaders. They are incredibly enthusiastic regarding their objectives and aims. They are aware of their needs and work diligently to meet them. Their enthusiasm is both irresistible and highly motivating. They are extremely committed to achieving their goals and also assist others in achieving theirs.

Enthusiastic executives boost productivity and ensure that employees remain focused on their vision. Enthusiasm aids leaders in instilling motivation in their representatives and in achieving the ideal vision.

Chapter 13: Mission Of A Leader

What is leadership's purpose? Certainly, the answer to this query is influenced by ethics, values, hopes, and distinctive worldviews. We tend to respond to this query based on what is important to us, which makes it an effective reflection of our internal understanding of why leaders do what they do. The purpose of leadership should ideally be reflected in our daily actions.

Every effective leader has a leadership-related mission. The purpose of your leadership should not be confused with the mission statement or corporate vision. The purpose is a distinctly private matter that centers around how you define yourself in the context of the situation. Our purposes are the ones that shape our leadership style and define who we are as individuals. Consider the instances when you were in a position of leadership and ask yourself: How did you envision leading the project?

What feedback do you believe your peers would have provided regarding your leadership?

How have you made your coworkers feel?

What personal objectives have you set?

Your responses to these queries will provide some perspective from which to work backwards. You can then begin to develop and refine your leadership purpose. Be aware that accomplishing this objective is not simple! You must be willing to accept responsibility for the broad picture (Dickson, n.d.). Remember that you are merely human and that it is acceptable to make errors. Effective leadership is ultimately a learning process.

Understanding Leadership Driven by Purpose

Leadership driven by a sense of purpose pays dividends. According to research, consumers view purpose-driven brands more favorably, resulting in brand loyalty (Bulgarella, 2018). Yet there can be a disconnect between what a leader perceives their purpose to be and what they actually do.

The objective is not restricted to creating a brand distinctive. In a business context, it can demonstrate the evolution of the organization. At its most fundamental, the purpose of an organization merely describes its aspirations. The mission of a business provides insight into its development. Some businesses seek to maintain the status quo, projecting a culture that is obsessed with results, hierarchy, and authority. On the opposite extreme of the continuum are organizations with more expansive perspectives that prioritize innovation. The position of an organization along this continuum would be determined by its mission. A closer examination of the mission statement may reveal useful clues. The objective must be divorced from the organization's current culture; otherwise, it will be inauthentic.

Leaders with a strong sense of purpose inspire improved performance from their employees. Research revealed even more remarkable and extensive advantages. Overall, purpose-driven businesses were found to have higher innovation and employee retention rates than their competitors. In addition, the research revealed that executives who had a clear understanding of their purpose were twice as likely to find significance in their work. A dearth of comprehension of what purpose actually entails is one of the greatest obstacles to this. Purpose is a relatively vague term. One individual might characterize it as resolve or determination. One individual may cite intentions or objectives as examples of purpose. It could be something entirely different, so a clearer understanding of the purpose is beneficial.

Chapter 14: Advantages And Disadvantages

Overflow is not something you acquire; it is something you must earn. Possibly one of the greatest gifts you can give yourself is the awareness and appreciation of the abundance and splendor in your life. This mindfulness will inspire a higher level of appreciation, and you should consider this movement routine. In fact, excess consciousness and appreciation are inextricably linked.

The Positive And Negative

The advantages of living a prosperous life.

By implication, overflow could imply copious. However, it also implies completion, which is the totality of the psyche and appreciation. Indeed, if you are experiencing an extraordinary abundance in your life, you should be grateful. The more you feel, think, and express gratitude, the more you will attract and accomplish things for which you are grateful.

The greater your awareness or consciousness of how abundant your life genuinely is.

The greater your appreciation, the healthier your chakras, energy bodies, and thus your physical body will be.

The Deficiencies

The disadvantage, however, is that certain prosperous individuals will frequently focus more on their happiness and will frequently boast about their significance.

This is one of the disadvantages of having a bountiful life, as people tend to fuel their eager inner self. Certainly, this is not true for all individuals.

Some are egotistical rather than appreciative of what they have in daily life; they generally seek more without considering the possibility that they are influencing another individual.

At this time, here is an exam for everyone: Why don't you think less about yourself and more about the interests and prosperity of others? Isn't this a far cry from being grateful for everything you have in life, achieving abundance, and being prosperous?

Keep in mind that narcissism, self-indulgence, and various forms of childishness will lead you down the path to misery.

If you genuinely want to live a long, happy, and fulfilling life, you must learn to appreciate and focus on your family members. You will become more joyful if you focus on trying to make other people happy and optimistic. Give, and you will receive. It is actually an infinite and never-ending circle. Giving and receiving is a way of existence.

Happiness versus misery? Altruism or egoism? Which will you choose? Without affection, individuals cannot experience genuine happiness. Without affection, the path to profound happiness is blocked, and obscurity envelops individuals. Joy is not contingent on serving oneself or seeking material gains. You can experience an abundance of love and happiness if you appreciate your existence and what it offers.

Chapter 15: Is Leadership An Easy Task?

As stated previously, the simple answer is no. Leadership is a delicate balancing act that requires you to don a million hats every day. Leadership is fraught with contradictions, and only those who are accustomed to multitasking will be able to rise to the occasion. This section will list some of the most prevalent challenges and contradictions that leaders, particularly women leaders, confront in the modern era. These are not intended to frighten you away from leadership, but rather to prepare you for future leadership responsibilities.

Be Optimistic but Present in the Present

The term "visionary" is frequently associated with leadership, but what does it actually mean? A visionary is someone who can envision a future reality and who, through their innovations, appears to be able to predict and influence the future. Frequently, they invent cutting-edge technologies or introduce novel political concepts that impel society forward. Visionaries are perpetually focused on the future and strive to overcome mental limitations in pursuit of innovative ideas and challenges. These are essential characteristics for innovators, entrepreneurs, and leaders. If you aspire to be a strong leader, you should cultivate visionary qualities that will keep your organization and initiatives innovative.

However, there is a disadvantage to being too futuristic. You can become overly preoccupied with the future and lose sight of the present. There is a time and a place for looking to the future, but it is easy to neglect current initiatives in favor of future ones. It's also simple to fall victim to "shiny object syndrome," which occurs when you begin to prioritize something new over something essential. Shiny object syndrome is the tendency to jump from project to project without committing to anything for the long term. Therefore, it can detract from the original objective of becoming a wonderful leader. It can also cause confusion among your team, which is working on the initial set of plans. As a leader, you must create a balance between the future and the present by dividing your focus between what your company and team require now and what they may do in the future.

Be Authoritative while Appealing

No one desires to be the cruel employer. At some point in our lives, we have all had a boss who was unfair or excessively punitive. If you've had negative experiences with overly authoritative supervisors in the past, it can be tempting to emphasize likeability as your primary leadership characteristic. It's enjoyable to be the fun boss, but it can be lonely at the top, so focusing on your likability in the workplace can boost your social self-esteem. Many female bosses aspire to be well-liked because they are frequently criticized if they are perceived as being too harsh, bossy, or even bitchy if they are too authoritative. This focus on likeability will be rewarded by your team in the form of employees who are more willing to go the extra mile for you, as well as feedback that you are a "cool boss" or "fun and nice." From this perspective, there is much to be said for seeking employee approval.

However, likability often has a diminishing return. There are several ways in which being too charming and insufficiently authoritative as a manager can backfire. Consider the television program The Office, specifically the UK version, in which David Brent is so concerned with his team's approval that he actively ignores his leadership responsibilities and is eventually fired. As a result of their apparent incompetence, these types of "cool bosses" frequently end up neglecting their responsibilities as leaders, leading to a decline in their employees' admiration and respect. If your priority is to be liked, you may end up allowing employees to miss deadlines or ignoring those who arrive late, resulting in a decline in your company's overall productivity. You may also establish a precedent for poor behavior, signaling to your team that they can get away with whatever they want to do because you have never stated otherwise. The second aspect of the "David Brent problem" is that trying too hard to be liked may not work with certain team members. They may perceive a transparent attempt to gain their favor, prefer a more professional working environment, and react with skepticism if a teacher attempts too hard to relate to them. Attempting to be liked could make you appear desperate for approbation, thereby undermining your authority and resulting in a general loss of respect. Therefore, while maintaining likeability can be advantageous, it should also have a limit.

As stated in Chapter 1, setting boundaries with your team is the most effective method for managing this challenge. Idealistically, you should maintain your team's respect and the authority you've earned as a leader. Consider methods of being likable that do not entail laxity in the workplace. For instance, you can assert your authority while remaining approachable by scheduling check-in meetings with employees whose performance is subpar and by recognizing their minor victories. This indicates that you are not accepting the behavior but are also not punishing them, resulting in a relationship that keeps you in control of the company culture and portrays you as a mentor who wants to help them improve. Taking the time to celebrate minor victories with them is motivating and demonstrates that you appreciate their effort. The best way to walk this tightrope between establishing acceptable behavior and gaining your team's favor may be to employ these types of likability and authority strategies.

A excellent leader must be an effective communicator. Simply communicating is insufficient. Your communications must achieve the intended outcome.

Communication that is clear, concise, and open is essential for effective leadership. Without effective communication, followers can become perplexed and misguided. Frequent communication typically indicates to followers that they are valued and that their requirements are a priority. Communication that is clear and concise can prevent misunderstandings.

Knowing the thoughts of the leadership will help adherents believe and trust the decisions made. Open communication facilitates a productive dialogue between employees and management.

The leader must ensure that his words effectively convey his meaning and purpose. It is essential to enable followers to believe they are part of a team and contributing to the accomplishment of common goals.

The leader is a member of a cohesive team, but he is the one in control. The leader understands the objective and guides the team toward it through effective communication.

Good leaders are efficient in their communications. They convey the information that keeps everyone informed and enables subordinates to make more informed decisions. Communication that is unnecessary is kept to a minimum.

If adherents comprehend the organization's mission and objectives, they can contribute to teamwork more effectively. Followers are exceptionally skilled. They can make the work environment challenging or simple.

Effective communication encourages followers to support the team's objectives. This allows them to contribute to the team's and organization's success. Leaders and adherents must be aware of the mission. Keeping everyone informed facilitates their participation and cooperation in attaining shared objectives.

Poor communication can lead to frustration, improper procedure implementation, and apathy. When leaders communicate plainly, the response and feedback will be significantly more beneficial and focused on the issues that must be resolved. Good communication is bidirectional and frequently requires attentive listening from both leaders and subordinates.

Good leaders are humble communicators. Instructions that are delivered in a severe and demanding manner are typically ineffective. To avoid confusion, verbal instructions should be succinct and frequently accompanied by written confirmation.

When communicating with individuals or other businesses in the modern workplace, it is also necessary to be culturally sensitive. It is especially crucial if you operate in a global marketplace. In a culturally diverse environment, choose your words with care, as they frequently have different connotations across cultures.

Good leaders encourage subordinates to provide suggestions and feedback. The most effective communication maximizes clarity and cooperation by being two-way. Communication both up and down the chain of command is frequently the key to attaining shared objectives.

Leaders must not only communicate with their employees about the task, but also about the organization, its purpose, and the team's role in the organization's mission. Knowledge assists employees in relating to their jobs and the organization as a whole. Employees want to know the purpose of their work and how it contributes to the final outcome.

Leaders assist team members in understanding their roles within the organization, their significance, and potential futures. To excite employees about their work, effective leaders portray a plausible picture of the future. A compelling storyteller can convey employees into a work environment and organizational possibilities that will inspire them to give their all to the team and the organization.

Chapter 16: Fundamentals For Creating A Healthy Corporate Culture

Establishing trust with your employees should be a fundamental and continuous goal for every leader in an organization. In a professional setting, there must be trust between leaders and employees so that difficult conversations are constructive and everyone has a sense of mutual respect and comprehension of the organization's mission and objectives.

Create security

Before an employee can have confidence in their team leader, they must first feel secure in their presence. In a broader sense, we can say that employees will leave a company if they do not feel secure or supported there. When an employee's emotional health, sense of self, or livelihood are threatened by their work environment, they cannot perform to the best of their ability.

3. Protect Liberty

Freedom can be defined as the capacity to speak, think, and act freely. This does not imply that there are no limits or accountability, especially within the context of an organization, but it does mean that employees are free to express their individuality and make their own decisions without fear of being judged or punished.

4. Foster Collaboration

This principle is optional because not all organizations are designed to support extensive collaboration. However, you can promote collaboration by hosting ideation sessions or by establishing a channel for employees to express their concerns and provide feedback.

5. Become People-Centered People-centered organizations value the exchange of ideas, socialization, employee wellness, and the provision of numerous opportunities for growth and development within the organization. Essentially, every aspect of the organization is designed to make employees' work lives more pleasurable and less stressful.

If you ask employees what they value most about their jobs, many will say that they value knowing that they make a difference every day. It is the responsibility of leaders to create a positive work environment in which the company's vision, mission, and values assist employees feel connected to the organization and accountable for achieving its objectives.

Chapter 17: The New Assessment Tool

When Robin described my internal architecture based on my birth information, I was astounded and captivated by the possibilities. She pointed out areas of my personality where conditioning is likely to manifest and how to counteract this. In that instant, I realized why I had avoided Human Design for so many years: I was not prepared to receive it because I lacked the time to research it in depth. My design is fascinated by information. But this was the instrument I desired.

In 1987, Human Design was initially transferred into Ra, a reluctant mystic. It was explained to him that this information was important for everyone, but particularly for parents who want to support their children. Understanding their children's blueprint could assist parents in recognizing their children for who they are and in determining how to help them flourish. Human Design is a new application based on ancient technologies such as astrology, the I Ching, and the Kabbalah, as well as modern understanding from quantum physics. It acknowledges the inherent brilliance and perfection of each individual, as well as any obstacles they may face. This definitive guide is a map - a blueprint - for our potential. The Human Design chart examines our operating system in its complexity. It categorizes humanity into five Types, each with its optimal Strategy for life success. In addition, it displays each individual's unique Authority, or decision-making process, and Profile, or learning approach. There are additional elements or layers, such as Gates, Channels, and the Planets, each of which reveals deeper levels of comprehension of who we are and how we navigate the world.

After my encounter with Robin, I enrolled in her training and began my Human Design voyage. It completely captivated me. I received downloads as I viewed charts while being captivated by the information. I marveled at the accuracy of the charts I generated of my family and acquaintances when I was fully engrossed in the process. At one point, I examined Yolanda's chart and exclaimed, "That's not Yolanda." I was surprised at my own intelligence – how did I know this? I was comparatively inexperienced with this method, but I trusted my intuition and called her to inquire about her birth time. She stated that she was delivered in an ambulance en route to the hospital, so her actual birth time was likely before 5:00 a.m.

After asking her a few inquiries, I determined that her birth time was 4:48.

Now, after working with more than a hundred clients, no one has ever stated, "This doesn't sound like me." The majority of them report feeling genuinely seen and acknowledged. Human Design has been the missing link in my leadership practice. While supervising teams in the business world and, later, the spiritual world, I frequently wished I had a window into how people operated. Since learning about Human Design, my work with them has reached an entirely new level.

Career Route

When establishing objectives, consider your long-term career path. Consider your optimal professional position and the qualifications or skills required to attain it. You must align your personal objectives to give yourself the opportunity to acquire the necessary skills. This also increases the motivation necessary to adhere to your plan.

It is essential that you reevaluate your professional circumstances every few months or years, as it is not uncommon for people's desires for a significant life to alter well into their professional careers. Ask yourself if your current job is satisfying and rewarding, and if it allows you to achieve financial independence and stability. If this is the case, then you are on the correct path, so congratulations!

In contrast, if you feel that your job no longer provides you with the initial gratification of knowing that what you do is useful or rewarding, it may be time to reevaluate your priorities and look elsewhere for better opportunities.

Ultimately, your progress and development will be dictated by your candor and transparency regarding your accomplishments.

The Big Picture Is Crucial

Productivity and skill are crucial characteristics of a successful manager. However, advancement in your professional career is not limited to productivity and skill alone. You must understand the experiences and skills necessary to advance in your selected field. Participate in professional seminars and educational opportunities whenever possible, regardless of your objective. For you to ascend the corporate hierarchy, you must engage in ongoing education. It is not, however, about becoming complacent in your managerial function. It is essential to perform the task to the utmost of one's ability. When pursuing career advancement, keeping the larger picture in mind will enable you to develop the skills and motivation necessary to become the best manager possible.

Understand Achievement

While setting a goal, you should contemplate what success and accomplishment mean to you. Clearly, your definition of achievement will differ from that of your coworkers and teammates. This indicates that you will need to go beyond the SMART technique introduced earlier. You must consider and visualize the form that your triumph will take. What actions can be taken to achieve the flow state? What can you do to increase your productivity? Hold on to the visualization of the objective in order to find the motivation to continue. Once you have a clearer understanding of your definitions of success and accomplishment, it is easier to set goals that will enable you to attain them.

Check-Ins

After establishing an objective and beginning to work towards it, you will need regular check-ins to monitor your progress. Consequently, the objective must be measurable. Once per week, engage in self-reflection and assess your progress toward the objective. During that time, consider any necessary adjustments or solutions to the obstacles or difficulties you confront. More often than not, the objective can shift, necessitating adjustments to the plan. Similarly, regular check-ins provide greater insight into what you can do differently in the future to avoid similar obstacles. Monitoring your progress also enables you to keep your energy levels in control, allowing you to allocate your resources more effectively and efficiently toward achieving your objective.

Support

Have you ever questioned how celebrities manage to always appear flawless? They are supported by a team of professionals who pander to their needs and requirements. This is how they present themselves in the finest light. Similarly, if you wish to achieve success, you will require a support system or a team. Being surrounded by people who can assist you in your professional endeavors is the most effective method to achieve optimal performance. When attempting to accomplish an objective, the same is required. Even if you are the one emphasizing on increasing your productivity at work, you must also attend to other aspects of your life. Therefore, you require a support infrastructure.

Whether the group consists of comrades, coworkers, or even family, friends, and loved ones, they will all be useful. To exemplify this point, if you want to improve your golfing skills, you will need a coach to teach you the fundamentals and help you hone your abilities. Likewise, you need allies to accomplish your personal and professional objectives. Whether it is a network of professionals within or outside the organization, you must always construct a solid support system. They will provide you with fortitude and motivation when your reserves are low, allowing you to refocus your energy and concentrate on what truly matters. You can also seek their counsel. Knowing that you are not alone and that others are independently supporting you can enhance your confidence in ways you never could have imagined.

Comparison

Establishing goals at work equips you with the means to map out the larger objectives you wish to achieve. However, you will also need to prioritize other matters. This can become a source of distraction that unnecessarily heightens your tension levels, which can become overwhelming if not managed. As a result, you will need to compare what you are doing with what you should be doing periodically. In other words, placing "what is" and "what should be" side-by-side will assist you in evaluating your performance and determining how close you are to achieving your goals. Once you realize this, you will be able to take the necessary steps to prioritize duties that add value and significance to your life. Verify that your daily to-do list aligns with your established objectives. Increasing the number of activities that will bring you closer to your goals while minimizing distractions is a foolproof method to realize your vision.

Consider the Wins

It is common knowledge that administrators are typically occupied. Occasionally, you may feel as if you're occupied but have nothing to show for it. In such situations, reflecting on one's accomplishments can be difficult. This becomes even more difficult if you are facing obstacles that prevent you from attaining your objectives. However, even if you are currently struggling, you are probably doing some things accurately. This includes things that are working well for you and victories you have achieved. It serves you well to recall everything you have sacrificed and endured to reach your current position. You must record your accomplishments to motivate yourself to pursue your ambitions and objectives. Don't dwell on the things that are not going well for you; instead, count your benefits and be thankful for the ones that are.

Again, we're discussing the third key. You must agree to submit the next bullet point. This is a very brief passage. It is stated that change must be structured for numerous factors. But one is the functioning of the intellect. All are reinforced, and a new discipline is implemented to supplant old patterns. Dr. Henry Cloud is a wonderful individual. Listen, change must be structured for numerous reasons, including the way the brain functions.

The old pattern is reinforced, and a new discipline is introduced to replace it. While we are attempting to develop as professionals, we have taken up a number of ingrained habits. And in order to override these old patterns, we must introduce ourselves to some new discipline, as this is the only thing that will be able to do so.

I taught about the new and the old in the first grade. I am unable to revisit the first key during this particular lecture. I want you to return and read it again. I discuss either number one or the new throughout the entirety of key number one. However, why am I saying this? Why am I mentioning this?

I bring this up because, as professionals, as peers or specialists or whatever your title may be, we have acquired stale practices. And some of these opportunities are things I have observed for the past twenty-two years. If you are unaware, I have struggled with various substances for fourteen years. For the past fourteen years, I have been sober.

God bless all the medications I used to be dependent on. Nonetheless, I paid close heed during the entire fourteen years that I was abstinent, abstinent from all of those drugs, and sober. I prefer the phrase fourteen years. I maintain my sobriety.

I have spent the past fourteen years observing and researching a variety of teachers, directors, clinical supervisors, counselors, and recovery coaches. Moreover, I have observed that they all circulated the same types of materials. And I asked, why are they all disseminating identical materials?

It was evidence-based information, but it was outdated, and they were afraid to try something novel. Numerous individuals with years of experience in this discipline, for instance, do not want to accept the existence of multiple recovery pathways. Now, you are aware that this is true, but at some point they will have to introduce a new discipline to themselves in order to overcome the old pattern.

I trust you realize that you must be willing to submit. Now, the next paragraph point states, we become predictable if we do not surrender or change. Without giving up or transforming, we become predictable. This is why it is crucial that I say we are becoming predictable. I don't want to disrupt you. And discuss the character of the individual you are or the integrity of the individual you represent.

www.ingramcontent.com/pod-product-compliance
Lightning Source LLC
Chambersburg PA
CBHW050250120526
44590CB00016B/2291